Japan
Travel Journal

If found, please return to

____

____

About my trip

Name

Date of birth

Nationality

Country of residence

Travel period

Travel companions

I am traveling to Japan for the ___ time

I really want to go to Japan because

Things that fascinate me about Japan

This is how I imagine Japan

My bucket list

Places I want to visit

Food and drink I want to try

Sights I want to see

Experiences I want to have

Packing list

Category

Category

Category

Category

Category

Category

Category

Category

Budget

Item or experience	Budgeted	Spent

Item or experience	Budgeted	Spent

Total budgeted **Total spent**

Japan
at a glance

Main islands

Hokkaido
approx. 6 million inhabitants

Honshu
approx. 104 million inhabitants

Shikoku
approx. 4 million inhabitants

Kyushu
approx. 13 million inhabitants

Okinawa Archipelago
approx. 1.4 million inhabitants

Hokkaido
Sapporo
Hakodate
Aomori
Hachinohe
Morioka
Pacific
Ocean
Sendai
Sado
Niigata
Fukushima
Honshu
Nagano
Takayama
Tokyo
goya
Yokohama
Okinawa
Prefecture
Kyushu
Yakushima
Amami
Okinawa
Ishigaki
Miyako
N
0 km 200
0 miles 200

Getting to know Japan

About the country

Japan is an island nation covering an **area** of 378,000 km^2 (146,000 miles^2) with a **population** of 127 million people.

There are **four main islands** – Honshu, Hokkaido, Shikoku, and Kyushu – and over 6,000 smaller islands that stretch around 3,000 km (1,900 miles) from the far north to the Okinawa Islands in the south. The Okinawa Archipelago is sometimes counted among the main islands. The country is divided into 47 administrative units called prefectures.

Tokyo is the **capital** of Japan and its largest city. It serves as the nation's political, economic, and cultural center, known for its blend of traditional landmarks and modern architecture.

The nation operates as a **parliamentary monarchy**, with the emperor serving as the symbol and de facto head of state, residing in Tokyo. The government system is rooted in the 1947 constitution.

The Japanese **flag** features a large red circle on a white background. It is called *Hinomaru*, meaning "sun disc."

While we refer to the country as Japan in English, the **local name** for the nation is *Nippon* (or *Nihon*), meaning "the sun's origin". Japanese is the **official language** and the main **currency** is the yen.

The **time zone** is Japan Standard Time (JST), which is UTC+9 hours.

Main islands

From stunning landscapes to vibrant cities, each of the main islands offers a unique charm, culture, and experience.

HONSHU

As Japan's largest island, Honshu is home to the bustling capital Tokyo, alongside lively cities like Kyoto, Osaka, and Hiroshima. It also offers iconic natural beauty, including Mount Fuji.

HOKKAIDO

The second-largest and northernmost of the main islands, Hokkaido draws in travelers for its unique natural landscapes and numerous national parks. The island is also home to the indigenous Ainu people.

SHIKOKU

The smallest and least populated of the main islands, Shikoku provides a tranquil escape. It's famous for its historic 88 Temple Pilgrimage and the art haven of Naoshima island.

KYUSHU

This island is characterized by its active volcanoes, geothermal vents, and many hot springs, alongside vibrant cities such as Fukuoka and Nagasaki.

OKINAWA ARCHIPELAGO

This island chain is known for white-sand beaches, coral reefs, and unique island culture. It is also recognized for the exceptionally long lifespans of its residents, classifying it as a "Blue Zone."

Etiquette

Familiarizing yourself with Japanese etiquette can really make your trip smoother and more enjoyable. Don't worry, you're not expected to be perfect right away, but showing that you're trying to respect the local customs will go a long way.

SHOES

Shoes are always taken off when visiting someone's home and anywhere there are *tatami* mats (the straw and reed mats on which people eat and sleep). However, rather than going barefoot, you'd usually wear socks (or sometimes slippers), so remember to pack a fresh pair when going out if you're not already wearing any. You may also be required to remove your shoes in *izakayas* (traditional pubs).

PUBLIC BATHS AND HOT SPRINGS

It is important to observe a few rules when visiting public baths *(sentō)* and hot springs *(onsen)*. Wash thoroughly before entering the water – this is typically done while seated in a shower area. Your hair must not touch the water, so remember to bring a hair tie if needed. It is polite to keep noise levels low to maintain a peaceful atmosphere. If you have tattoos, check in advance whether entry is allowed, as they are not accepted everywhere.

DINING

When using chopsticks, avoid pointing them at others, waving them around, or using them to stab food. Do not pass food from one set of chopsticks to another and never stick chopsticks upright in a bowl of rice, as this looks like a funeral ritual. When eating from a rice bowl, hold the bowl in one hand and bring the chopsticks to your mouth with the other, so if any food falls from the chopstick, it will land back in the bowl.

MONEY AND SHOPPING

Money is rarely exchanged from hand to hand. Instead, you'll typically find a small tray where you can place your payment. Tipping is not customary and will likely be returned if offered.

When trying on clothes in stores, you may be offered bags or cloths; these are used to cover your face to prevent makeup from getting on the garments.

Japanese writing

Written Japanese is a fascinating combination of three distinct systems:

KANJI

These are Chinese ideograms, representing concepts or words.

HIRAGANA

One of two syllabaries, Hiragana is primarily used for grammatical endings and native Japanese words.

KATAKANA

This is the other syllabary, and is mainly used for foreign words and names.

Japanese text is traditionally read from top to bottom, with columns progressing from right to left. However, you'll also increasingly see the western-style left-to-right writing system in use.

Useful words and phrases

Here are a few useful words and phrases that you'll likely come across while planning your trip and when traveling around Japan. Mastering even a few basic expressions can greatly improve your day-to-day interactions and make navigating easier while exploring the country.

COMMUNICATION ESSENTIALS

Hello ***Konnichiwa***

How are you? ***Ogenki desu ka?***

Good bye ***Sayonara***

Thank you ***Arigato***

No, thank you ***Kekko desu***

Yes/No ***Hai/Iie***

Cheers! ***Kampai!***

Delicious! ***Oishii!***

Excuse me/Sorry ***Sumimasen***

Can you help me? ***Chotto tetsudatte itadakemasen ka?***

Do you speak English? ***Eigo o hanesemasu ka?***

I don't understand ***Wakarimasen***

I don't know ***Shirimasen***

Where is the restroom? ***Otearai/otoire wa doko desu ka?***

IN AN EMERGENCY

Help! ***Tasukete!***

Stop! ***Tomete!***

Call a doctor! ***Isha o yonde kudasai!***

Call an ambulance! ***Kyukyusha o yonde kudasai!***

Call the police! ***Keisatsu o yonde kudasai!***

Fire! ***Kaji!***

Police box ***koban***

Where is the hospital? ***Byoin wa doko ni arimasu ka?***

PLACES TO EAT AND DRINK

Local bar or pub ***izakaya***

Traditional inn ***ryokan***

Noodle stall ***ramen-ya***

Restaurant ***resutoran/ryori-ya***

Coffee shop ***kissaten/kafe***

FOOD

bento boxes for train travel ***ekiben***

crab ***kani***

egg ***tamago***

fish (raw) ***sashimi***

fried tofu ***abura-age***

fruit ***kudamono***

meat ***niku***

potato ***jagaimo***

rice (cooked) ***gohan***

sushi (mixed) ***gomoku-zushi***

vegetables ***yasai***

DRINKS

beer ***biru***

coffee (hot) ***hotto-kohi***

cola ***kora***

green tea ***ocha***

iced coffee (black) ***aisu-kohi***

iced coffee (with milk) ***aisu-ore***

tea (western style) ***kocha***

water ***mizu***

SIGHTSEEING AND SHOPPING

art gallery ***bijitsukan***

bookstore ***honya***

castle ***shiro/jo***

city center ***machi no chushin***

convenience store ***konbini***

department store ***depato***

gardens ***teien/niwa***

hot spring ***onsen***

information office ***annaijo***

open-air hot spring ***rotenburo***

public bath ***sento***

market ***ichiba***

monastery ***shudo-in***

mountain ***yama/san***

museum ***hakubutsukan***

palace ***kyuden***

park ***koen***

shopping area ***shoppingu-gai***

shrine ***jinja/jingu/gu***

temple ***otera/tera/dera/ji***

Useful information

Entry

For detailed and up-to-date information on visas, entry into Japan, and customs regulations, consult your nearest Japanese embassy or check Japan's Ministry of Foreign Affairs website *(www.mofa.go.jp)*. European Union nationals and citizens of the UK, US, Canada, Australia, New Zealand, and many other countries can visit Japan for up to 90 days without applying for a visa before travel. Your passport must be valid for the length of your stay and you need a blank page for the visa stamp that you'll get on arrival.

While in Japan, you must carry ID (such as your passport or residence card) with you at all times. A photocopy of your passport photo page and visa (if applicable) should suffice.

Prepaid IC cards

It's a good idea to use a prepaid IC (Integrated Circuit) card for travel throughout Japan. These are rechargeable, contactless smart cards that are mainly used for public transport. They can also be used for some other purchases that accept electronic payments.

You can purchase these cards at major airports or from ticket machines located in larger train stations. A deposit is required for the card, which is refunded upon its return. Alternatively, you may choose to keep the card as a souvenir.

Using an IC card can streamline your travel significantly. They are accepted for most journeys on Japan Rail (JR) lines, as well as other train operators, subways, and buses, eliminating the need to purchase individual tickets for each ride. Additionally, they can be used for payments on purchases at some convenience stores and vending machines.

While many regions offer their own IC cards (featuring unique names or mascots), most are generally valid nationwide. The main providers are Pasmo *(www.pasmo.co.jp)* and Suica *(www.jreast.co.jp)*. Suica also offers a specialized Welcome Card designed for tourists. Further details on the specific cards can be found on the providers' official websites.

Japan Rail Pass

If you're planning to travel extensively across Japan, especially on the *Shinkansen* (Japan's high-speed trains), you should look into purchasing a Japan Rail Pass. It can offer significant cost savings compared to buying individual train tickets for all your trips.

It is crucial to note that you must buy this pass before you leave your home country, as it is no longer available for purchase within Japan. For all the details on how it works and whether it's right for your travel plans, refer to the official website *(www.japanrailpass.net)*.

Wi-Fi

It's not always easy to find Wi-Fi in Japan. Some hotels offer pocket Wi-Fi or a smartphone with internet access for their guests.

It's best to check with your phone provider about data usage in Japan before your trip. Alternatively, you can consider buying a second SIM card or renting a pocket Wi-Fi device directly at the airport in Japan.

Power

Be sure to pack a power adapter for your electronic devices. Japan's voltage is 100 volts, and the frequency differs slightly between regions – 50 hertz in eastern Japan and 60 hertz in western Japan. The power outlets are type A and B.

Travelers with specific requirements

Japan offers good infrastructure for people with limited mobility, or visual or hearing impairments.

You'll increasingly find *Tamokuteki toire* (barrier-free toilets) in places like train stations, department stores, and even on high-speed trains. These facilities are wheelchair-accessible and equipped with an emergency button for assistance.

For more detailed information on disabled access and facilities across the country, refer to Accessible Japan *(www.accessible-japan.com)*.

LGBTQ+

LGBTQ+ visitors are unlikely to encounter problems in Japan. It's worth noting that public displays of affection, whether between heterosexual or same-sex couples, are uncommon in Japanese culture. Utopia Asia *(www.utopia-asia.com)* is a useful resource for more information on Japan's LGBTQ+ scene.

Emergencies and medical care

If you experience a crime, report it within 24 hours to the nearest police station and take ID with you. Contact your embassy if your passport is stolen, or in the event of a serious crime or accident.

Japan has a world-class health system, but medical expenses can be extremely high, so it is important to arrange comprehensive medical insurance for your trip. If you are sick while in Japan, consult a doctor at a local clinic; for minor problems, see a pharmacist.

Vaccinations are not currently required for entry into the country. However, vaccination against encephalitis is advised if you're planning on staying for over a month or are visiting rural areas.

EMERGENCY NUMBERS

Fire department and ambulance: **119**
Police: **110**
Coast guard: **118**

Japan across the seasons

Though most famed for its springtime cherry blossoms, Japan is a country that transforms beautifully with each turn of the calendar. From vibrant summer events to stunning autumn colors and serene winter landscapes, there's a unique charm awaiting visitors in every season.

Spring

When spring arrives in Japan, there's one undeniable star: the cherry blossom *(sakura)*. As the blossom repaints the country a palette of pinks, everyone's eyes are on the trees. Even before the first buds appear, forecasts and predictions eagerly announce when the bloom will begin in different regions.

In Tokyo, a specific "indicator tree" is chosen for observation, and the moment its first blossoms open, Tokyo's cherry trees are officially declared "in bloom." You can track this "blossom front" through news reports and apps, letting you know exactly where in the country the beautiful pink hues are lighting up.

During this season, blossom viewing, or *hanami*, is a beloved activity for many locals and tourists alike. The blossom's fleeting existence epitomizes the concept of *mono no aware*, which is the beauty of impermanence.

Attending one of the many cherry blossom festivals or enjoying a picnic beneath the flowering trees is a truly unforgettable experience, making springtime a particularly magical time to visit Japan.

Beyond cherry blossoms, the season offers much more to admire; plum trees bloom beautifully, and various other celebrations take place, including Golden Week (April 29–May 6), which is a collection of national holidays that brings a lively buzz to the country.

Summer

Summertime in Japan is peak festival season, with many celebrations and spectacular fireworks displays taking place all over the country.

Depending on the region you're in, this time of year can be very hot and humid. You'll find an array of cooling seasonal food and refreshments on offer, such as *kakigōri* (shaved ice topped with fruit-flavored syrup and condensed milk), *sōmen* (chilled noodles), and cold green tea. To escape the heat, locals often flock to places like Hokkaido in the far north, where winter ski areas such as Niseko provide a cooler summer setting for hiking and other outdoor pursuits.

The rainy season *(tsuyu)* runs from June to mid-July, and typhoons can occur between May and October, with August and September being the peak months; however, the weather forecasts for this are generally quite reliable.

Fall

In fall, the vibrant transformation of nature takes center stage across the country. The countless trees ablaze with brilliant yellow and red foliage, known as *kōyō*, are an extraordinary sight.

While there aren't dedicated *kōyō* festivals, like there are for cherry blossoms, many people eagerly visit parks and mountains to marvel at the changing leaves during fall. The bright yellow leaves along Ginkgo Avenue in Meiji-jingu Gaien Park are a highlight in Tokyo, as are the reds and yellows of Rikugien Garden. In Kyoto, the deep-red maples at Eikando Temple have people queuing for hours to see them.

Beyond enjoying nature, during fall you can take in major events like Kyoto's Jidai Matsuri in late October, which features a parade of more than 2,000 people representing figures from Japanese history, and the Grand Autumn Festival held in mid-October at Nikko's UNESCO-designated Toshogu Shrine, which includes *yabusame* horseback archery displays.

Winter

Winter in many parts of Japan can be cold, making a comforting soak in a hot spring *(onsen)* or public bath *(sentō)* an incredibly inviting activity. You'll also find that hot plum wine *(umeshu)* and hearty dishes like curries and stews become especially popular, drinks in vending machines switch from cold to hot, and at night, the catchy jingle of sweet potato trucks can be heard.

Festive winter illuminations light up cities nationwide around Christmas and New Year, and special culinary traditions like *osechi-ryōri* (symbolic New Year foods) appear in ornate lacquered boxes on dining tables across Japan.

Hatsumōde – the first shrine or temple visit of the new year – is a time where people pray for good fortune for the year ahead. Many people also gather to watch the *hatsuhinode*, the first sunrise of the year.

Once the holidays are over, there are plenty of other events to enjoy over the season, such as the Sapporo Snow Festival in Hokkaido, where giant ice sculptures are created around the city.

PUBLIC HOLIDAYS

Jan 1 New Year's Day
2nd Mon, Jan Coming of Age Day
Feb 11 National Foundation Day
Feb 23 Emperor's Birthday
Mar 20/21 Vernal (Spring) Equinox
Apr 29 Showa Day
May 3 Constitution Memorial Day
May 4 Greenery Day
May 5 Children's Day
3rd Mon, Jul Marine Day
Aug 11 Mountain Day
3rd Mon, Sep Respect for the Aged Day
Oct 22/23 Autumnal Equinox
2nd Mon, Oct Sports Day
Nov 3 Culture Day
Nov 23 Labor Thanksgiving Day

Souvenirs and lucky charms

As you journey through Japan, you can collect a wide variety of souvenirs. Among the most special keepsakes are *eki* stamps, a unique feature across the country that you'll notice on your travels. See below to find out what they're all about – and what other lucky charms exist, too.

Eki stamps

Eki stamps – also known as *sutanpu* – are charming, collectible rubber stamps you'll find throughout all of Japan.

Originally introduced at train stations (*eki* means station), these stamps were designed as fun, memorable keepsakes for travelers. Today, their popularity has spread far beyond railway hubs. You can now spot custom stamps at airports, museums, tourist information centers, and various popular attractions. They're typically placed in entry areas or near ticket counters.

The origin of these stamps lies in Buddhist and Shinto pilgrimages, which still play a significant role in Japan's spiritual life today. Pilgrims traditionally visit temples and shrines, where they receive a stamp – called *goshuin* – as proof of completing their pilgrimage. These stamps are artistically crafted by the monks and usually show the seal and name of the site, and are made on individual sheets of paper. Starting from these pilgrimage stamps (which still exist today and aren't free), the practice spread into the railway world, with the growth of train stations and travel, and eventually throughout the entire country.

Eki stamps are usually free and uniquely designed. They might feature regional landmarks or interests, pop culture characters and mascots, landscapes, and of course, trains. Collecting them is great fun and a very special way to remember your trip. You'll find plenty of space to collect your stamps in this journal.

TIPS FOR STAMPING

1. There are some blogs online that list all the places where you can find *eki* stamps. Check out these lists during your planning to know where you can collect stamps.

2. If you can't find the stamps right away, you can ask local staff for help.

3. If possible, test the stamp on a separate sheet beforehand to get a nice result. Stamp evenly, without too much pressure.

4. You can also bring your own ink pad. That way, you can be sure you'll have ink for stamping in case the available pads are dried out or empty.

Lucky charms and talismans

Throughout Japan, you'll discover a fascinating array of lucky charms and talismans. These small, decorative items are believed to offer various forms of luck and protection, and they make popular souvenirs and gifts.

OMAMORI

These colorful silk pouches contain a piece of paper representing the power of a deity or the Buddha. They can be purchased at Buddhist temples or Shinto shrines and are meant to protect those who carry them. Their meanings can vary – some stand for health, others for financial success, and others for love and happiness. Interestingly, *Omamori* must never be opened and are said to lose their effectiveness after one year, when they should be returned to the temple where they were purchased to be burned as offerings.

DARUMA

These papier-mâché dolls, with no arms or legs, always stand back up thanks to the small weight at their base. *Daruma* represents Bodhidharma, the founder of Zen, and symbolizes perseverance and luck. The doll is sold with blank eyes – when you buy one, you make a wish or set a goal, and paint in one eye. Every time you see the one-eyed *daruma*, you're reminded of your goal or wish, so you don't lose sight of it. Once the wish is fulfilled, you paint in the other eye.

MANEKI-NEKO

These popular beckoning cat figurines are said to bring prosperity and good luck. The cat usually waves with one paw and holds a gold coin in the other.

ORIGAMI CRANE

The origami crane is also considered a bringer of good luck in Japan. According to legend, anyone who folds 1,000 of these birds will have a wish granted.

Culinary Japan

Japan's food culture is incredibly diverse, celebrated for fresh, seasonal ingredients, meticulous preparation, and beautiful presentation.

SUSHI AND SASHIMI

Considered Japan's unofficial national dish, the style of sushi served globally today developed into its modern form in Tokyo as early as the 18th century. Like sushi, sashimi (thin slices of raw fish) is often served with wasabi and soy sauce.

Sashimi is also a key ingredient in *kaiseki-ryōri*, a traditional tasting menu that represents the highest form of Japanese culinary art – a truly unique dining experience. This elaborate feast usually consists of ten to twelve courses, offered in special restaurants or *ryokan* (traditional Japanese inns). Each dish is made with high-quality seasonal ingredients, and is served on fine tableware as an edible work of art.

RAMEN

If you're looking for a quick, budget-friendly, and typically Japanese meal, a bowl of ramen is an excellent choice. The variations of this hearty, warming noodle soup are endless. You'll find different broths combined with various meats or vegetables, and a choice of noodles. The most well-known types include *soba* (buckwheat noodles), *udon* (thicker wheat flour noodles), and *ramen* (wavy wheat noodles of Chinese origin). Tip: slurping is allowed – it shows you're enjoying the soup and enhances the flavor.

STREET FOOD AND SNACKS

Japan is a paradise for all kinds of street food, such as *takoyaki* (octopus balls), *onigiri* (rice balls), *yakitori* (grilled skewers), and *tempura* (battered and fried foods).

And you'll find no shortage of snacks either: popular choices include rice crackers *(senbei)*, chips, *mochi* (rice cakes), and *wagashi* (traditional Japanese sweets carefully crafted into small edible artworks). You can easily find these and many more in convenience stores *(konbini)*, department stores, grocery stores, and the countless vending machines throughout Japan.

BENTO BOXES

While exploring supermarkets and grocery stores, you will likely come across bento boxes. These incredibly popular pre-packed meals come in countless varieties, but typically feature rice, a main item like fish, chicken, or meat, and an assortment of side dishes such as vegetables, pickles, or a mini omelet. All components are neatly arranged in separate compartments, making them perfect for a quick lunch break or a picnic in the park.

For train journeys, look out for *ekiben* – specially curated travel bentos available at train stations. These are often filled with regional ingredients, offering a unique taste of the area you're traveling through.

TEA

Just as sushi comes to mind when you think of Japanese food, green tea and matcha tea are the typical drinks.

Green tea plays a central role in daily life in Japan; you'll find it enjoyed hot or cold, and it's available in many varieties in trendy cafés and even from vending machines.

Matcha is a fine powder that is mixed with hot water and whisked with a bamboo brush. The aroma is both intense and flavorful. Matcha tea is famously used in tea ceremonies – a highly ritualized and formal tradition perfected over centuries to promote inner calm. These ceremonies can last several hours and offer a truly special Japanese cultural experience.

SAKE AND WHISKY

Interestingly, Japan's national drink isn't tea at all – it's sake. In Japan, it's called *nihonshu*, and early forms of this alcoholic beverage, made from fermented rice, were brewed in temples and shrines over 2,000 years ago. Today, there are more than 1,000 sake breweries across Japan.

Sake pairs wonderfully with Japanese food, offers less acidity than wine, and features that distinctive umami flavor.

Though Japanese whisky production is a relatively new craft, the country's whiskies consistently rank among the world's best, making Japan a fantastic destination for any whisky lover.

Religious Japan

In Japan, you'll encounter many shrines and temples, which represent the country's two main religions: Shintoism and Buddhism. Many Japanese people follow both religions and there's a strong tradition of mutual tolerance.

SHINTOISM

Shintoism is Japan's oldest religion. It has no single founder or holy scripture. At its core, Shinto (meaning "the Way of the Gods") is based on the belief that divinity, or *kami* (deities, nature spirits, and the souls of the deceased) can be found everywhere in nature – whether living, dead, or inanimate. A life lived in harmony and mutual respect with nature and others is central to this faith.

Shinto shrines are considered the homes of the *kami*, with each dedicated to a specific deity. For instance, Inari is one of the most well-known and beloved *kami*. You can often recognize Shinto shrines by the distinctive vermilion-colored *torii* gates at their entrance. These gates symbolically mark the transition from the everyday world to the sacred world.

When visiting a shrine, you typically begin by washing your hands at a stone water basin near the entrance as a sign of purification. From there, a stone path *(sandō)* leads to the *heiden* (offering hall), *haiden (*worship hall), and *honden* (main shrine), which houses the *kami*. Usually, only the *heiden* is accessible to visitors, with the main shrine reserved for priests. To respectfully get the *kami's* attention, you can ring a bell and clap your hands, and it's customary to throw a coin into the donation box.

BUDDHISM

Buddhism came to Japan in the 6th century CE from India, via China and Korea. It developed in Japan as a complement to the native Shinto religion, and the two have coexisted peacefully ever since. Buddhist teachings and morals are woven into many aspects of modern Japanese life, particularly the mental discipline emphasized in Zen Buddhism.

Zen is one of the most well-known schools of Buddhism. Its core elements are seated meditation and self-discipline. Zen's aesthetic simplicity and focus on essentials have had a significant influence on Japanese art and culture. This influence can be seen in garden design, tea ceremony rituals, and philosophical concepts like *wabi-sabi* (the beauty in imperfection) and *mono no aware* (an awareness of the transience of things).

Another branch of Buddhism is the Shingon school, which, like the Tendai school, is part of esoteric Buddhism in Japan. Founded in the 9th century by the monk Kukai, it incorporates elements like *mudras* (hand gestures) and mantra chanting.

Mount Koya *(Kōya-san)* is the holiest site of Shingon Buddhism and there, you'll find the symbolic red and white Konpon Daitō pagoda in the Danjo Garan temple complex. There were once around 1,000 temples on the mountain, but today, only 117 remain, as the rest have been lost to typhoons and fires over time.

When visiting a Buddhist temple, you'll usually first pass through a large main gate *(sanmon)*. At many of these gates, you'll notice statues of fearsome Nio guardians, who protect the temple from evil spirits. You may also spot statues of Jizo, the guardian deity – often depicted holding a pilgrim's staff in one hand and a wish-fulfilling jewel in the other.

At the center of the grounds is the main hall *(hondo)* which houses the principal image of the Buddha and an offering table. Prayer is done in quiet devotion, often kneeling before the altar. You may see many people dressed in white, the traditional attire for Buddhist pilgrims.

Entertaining Japan

From traditional theater, geisha, and sports to modern pastimes such as arcade gaming and karaoke, Japan offers up a world of entertainment for escaping the everyday. There is also a great appreciation for artisanal crafts, from bonsai and flower arranging to calligraphy and ceramics.

MANGA AND ANIME

With imaginative stories and beloved characters, manga and anime have introduced Japanese culture to people across the globe. You'll find numerous themed events and plenty of shops where you can buy merchandise and costumes for your favorite characters.

KAWAII

Kawaii – the culture of cuteness – is something you'll see everywhere in Japan. The most famous icon of this trend, Hello Kitty, was created in 1974 to join the cast of characters decorating the fashion and lifestyle products of the Sanrio company. Today, you can even find an entire train themed on this little white cat.

Many other businesses and institutions also create their own *kawaii*-inspired mascots, known as *yuru-kyara* – meaning "loose" or "relaxed" characters. You may also notice Japan's decorated manhole covers, which often depict regional attractions, festivals, historical events, and well-known characters.

SPORTS

While baseball and soccer are the most-watched sports on Japanese TV, the country has diverse sporting interests, with everything from rugby to martial arts *(bujutsu)*, which evolved from the military traditions of samurai.

Japan's two most famous martial arts styles are karate and judo, but there are many others such as *ninjutsu* (skills from the Ninja), *kendo* (the way of the sword), and *yabusame* (horseback archery), which can be seen at the Tsuwano Yabusame Festival in April.

Japan's national sport, sumo is believed to have originated as part of a harvest ritual for the gods. Every year, six 15-day grand sumo tournaments take place across Tokyo and the prefectures of Nagoya, Osaka, and Fukuoka.

THEATER

The exaggerated visuals and exciting atmosphere of traditional Japanese theater, such as the dramatic storylines of *kabuki* and *bunraku* puppet dramas, make for an unmissable experience. You can also find theater performances based on modern pop culture, and even western musicals and influences such as Shakespeare.

KARAOKE

Combining the casual feel of after-work drinks with the entertainment value of a sing-along, karaoke has its roots in *utagoe kissa* – singing cafés that were popular in the 1950s to 1970s. In Japan, it's a common team-bonding exercise and a way to let off steam. In any urban area of the country, you're likely to be spoilt for choice when it comes to karaoke joints.

CRAFTS

Japan's decorative arts can be found throughout the country, from galleries selling local crafts to world-renowned national collections. Many of these crafts are heavily guided by Shinto and Buddhist philosophies, balancing a meticulous attention to detail with finding the beauty in imperfection, and a love of nature.

You can find workshops to try your hand at traditional crafts, from lacquerwork and ceramics to origami and *ikebana* (the art of flower arranging). Calligraphy *(shodō)* also holds special significance in Japan – it is considered an art form, and reflects the pursuit of beauty and self-expression.

The journey begins

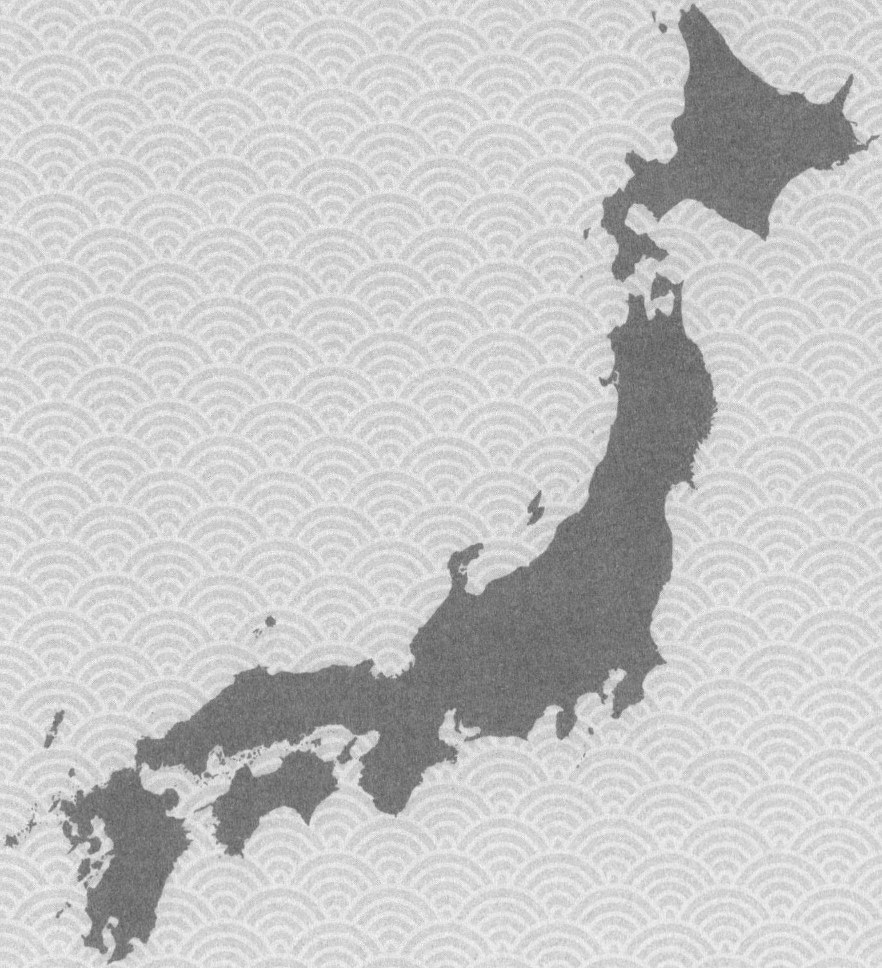

Mark your travel route on the map

First, I would like to

I'm most looking forward to

I definitely want to try

I hope

My plan for the week

Monday	Tuesday	Wednesday	Thursday

Friday	Saturday	Sunday

Accommodation details

Notes

What is your plan for today?

Day 1

Day 1

What did you experience today?

Use these pages to collect stamps, stickers, tickets, and other mementos.

Day 2

What is your plan for today?

Day 2

What would you recommend to others?

What is your plan for today?

Day 3

Day 3

What was the best thing you ate today?

What is your plan for today?

Day 4

Day 4

What did you learn today?

What is your plan for today?

Day 5

Day 5

Best conversation you had?

What is your plan for today?

Day 6

Day 6

What new thing did you try today?

Day 7

What is your plan for today?

Day 7

Who did you meet today?

My first week in Japan

What were your favorite moments?

My reviews

What

My review

/10

What

My review

/10

What

My review

/10

What

My review

/10

What

My review

/10

What

My review

/10

What

My review

/10

What

My review

/10

My plan for the week

Monday	Tuesday	Wednesday	Thursday

Friday	Saturday	Sunday

Accommodation details

Notes

What is your plan for today?

Day 8

Day 8

What did you experience today?

Day 9

What is your plan for today?

Day 9

What would you recommend to others?

What is your plan for today?

Day 10

What was the best thing you ate today?

What is your plan for today?

Day 11

What did you learn today?

What is your plan for today?

Day 12

Day 12

Best conversation you had?

What is your plan for today?

Day 13

What new thing did you try today?

Day 14

What is your plan for today?

Day 14

Who did you meet today?

My second week in Japan

What were your favorite moments?

My reviews

What

My review

/10

What

My review

/10

What

My review

/10

What

My review

/10

What

My review

/10

What

My review

/10

What

My review

/10

What

My review

/10

My plan for the week

Monday	Tuesday	Wednesday	Thursday

Friday	Saturday	Sunday

Accommodation details

Notes

What is your plan for today?

Day 15

Day 15

What did you experience today?

Day 16

What is your plan for today?

Day 16

What would you recommend to others?

What is your plan for today?

Day 17

Day 17

What was the best thing you ate today?

What is your plan for today?

Day 18

Day 18

What did you learn today?

What is your plan for today?

Day 19

Best conversation you had?

What is your plan for today?

Day 20

Day 20

What new thing did you try today?

Day 21

What is your plan for today?

Day 21

Who did you meet today?

My third week in Japan

What were your favorite moments?

My reviews

What

My review

/10

What

My review

/10

What

My review

/10

What

My review

/10

What

My review

/10

What

My review

/10

What

My review

/10

What

My review

/10

Published in Great Britain by Dorling Kindersley Limited, DK, 20 Vauxhall Bridge Road, London SW1V 2SA, UK
The authorised representative in the EEA is Dorling Kindersley Verlag GmbH. Arnulfstr.124, 80636 Munich, Germany
Published in the United States by DK Publishing, 1745 Broadway, 20th Floor, New York, NY 10019, USA

10 9 8 7 6 5 4 3 2 1
001-357985-Nov/2025

Adapted from: Reisetagebuch Japan
Originally published by Dorling Kindersley Verlag

Picture Credits
Cover images (front and back): Getty Images / iStock:
Digital Vision Vectors / Bernard Allum, Digital Vision Vectors / molotovcoketail

All interior pages: Getty Images / iStock:
Digital Vision Vectors / molotovcoketail (background pattern)

ISBN: 978 0 2418 0144 4
Printed and bound in Malaysia.

www.dk.com

MIX
Paper | Supporting responsible forestry
FSC™ C018179

This book was made with Forest Stewardship Council™ certified paper – one small step in DK's commitment to a sustainable future.
Learn more at
www.dk.com/uk/information/sustainability